# Skittle's Little Book of Kitten Wisdom

# Skittle's Little Book of Kitten Wisdom

## Skittle the Kitten
and K. Rose Quayle

Copyright © 2020 K. Rose Quayle

The moral right of this author has been asserted.

All rights reserved.
No part of this publication may be reproduced, stored in a retrieval system, or transmitted, in any form or by any means, without the prior permission in writing of the publisher, nor be otherwise circulated in any form of binding or cover other than that in which it is published and without a similar condition being imposed on the subsequent purchaser.

Cover art Copyright © 2020 K. Rose Quayle
Book design and production by K. Rose Quayle

Published by K. Rose Quayle
Pittsburgh, PA, United States of America

Skittle's Little Book of Wisdom is set in Georgia 12 pt. Cover is set in Beth Ellen 2 by Rob Jelinski Studios and California FB.
Photos by K. Rose Quayle, additional photos by A. Quayle

ISBN: 978-0-578-76192-3

In memory of Haley Adeleine,
the original "skittle" whose unwavering determination to move
despite her paralyzed legs gave her the speed of a kitten.

Hi! I'm Skittle!

As you can see, I'm a kitten and I came to live with my humans when I was 9 weeks old. I like to do all the usual kitten things like chasing my tail, getting into things I shouldn't and teasing the dog. But I also like to talk about mental health. Is that weird for a cat? I don't think so. I live in a house where mental health is a daily conversation in regard to humans *and* animals. And that's lucky for me, because cats can suffer from mental illnesses such as Post Traumatic Stress Disorder, Obsessive Compulsive Disorder, Depression, and Dementia just like humans can. So, if I ever have any problems, I know I'll be able to go right to my humans and talk about it.

Or meow about it.

Oh well, they'll get the idea!

In this little book I'm going to talk about some things I've learned about managing my mental health that might be helpful to you. You might think I don't know very much because I'm a not a human and I'm not very old. But cats are very observant creatures and kittens…well, let's just say we're all about having experiences and learning new stuff! So, if you turn the page, we'll get right to it.

*Love,* Skittle

*Boy was I having a bad day here!*

Or was I? You can have a positive effect on your mental health just by changing your thoughts around a little. If you've had a rotten day you can't just *think* it away, but you can change how you look back at it, so it doesn't have to ruin tomorrow. Let's try it! Look at the picture and notice how it looks like I've just thrown in the towel. Don't I look *so over it*? Now turn this book upside down and look again. Go ahead, I'll wait.

Now don't I look like I'm flying? I'm Super Skittle! So even though I had a bad day, I got through it like a superhero and I can do it again tomorrow. Just looking at a bad situation a different way can help train our brains to focus less on the negative, so we don't get stuck in it. It takes a little practice, but you've probably been a Super Skittle too and didn't even notice.

I bet your doctor has told you exercise is good for your body, but did you know exercise is great for your *mental health* too? It makes sense, doesn't it? Your mental health is all about your brain and how it regulates your feelings and thoughts. Your brain is part of your body, right? Well there you go!

Everybody is a little different about exercise. Some exercises work better for some and less for others. I like to run around my house and jump over the couch, it's pretty exhilarating stuff! But quiet exercises are good too. See my big round rug? It's *purrfect* for yoga! Try to get some daily form of exercise in, even if you do it while you watch television!

This is my big dog-brother, Orry.

He's big, smelly, and loud. But he's also my friend.

Friends are good for our mental health because they allow us to talk about things that are stressful and share things that are positive. While cats are rather solitary but don't mind company, humans are social creatures and need company. Don't sweat it if you've just got a few friends- or even one! Just one friend is all you need to help keep your brain in good order.

But what if you have a mental illness and you're looking for a friend? Well there's millions of others in the world living with mental illness too, so you already know there's people out there with something in common with you and they already have a good idea of what it's like to be you. Just start reaching out!

But don't put your paws on their plate. They might not like that.

Do you ever cry?

Maybe over something sad, maybe over something glad?

I was thinking of my family when I was a teeny tiny kitten, before I moved in with my family now. I love my new family but it's ok to miss my old one. Crying is something you humans are a little silly about. Did you know that scientists think when you cry, your body tries to balance itself? It goes sort of like this: you get upset or happy in some way and your heart and breathing speed up and get a little out of balance.

Then when you cry, your heart and breathing slow down and recalibrate. That's pretty neat to have your own built-in system to get things back in order, isn't it? And it feels good to your brain because it's a big release. That's why you can cry when things are really bad *or* really great!

So, is it bad to cry? No, silly humans! Next time you feel like it, sit down and have a cry. Just make sure you've got a box of tissues handy 'cos even my little kitten boogies are kinda gross.

Ever have a day when you're struggling, and it just seems like nothing is ever going to work out?

Or maybe a whole week? Or a *month*? You might not think I know a whole lot about that but believe me, kittens get down too. I mean, the whole world is so much bigger than me! I can't reach anything, and I fall off stuff and I always have to wait for my humans to get me what I want... it can be rough. But what I find helps is getting a daily dose of sunlight to keep my mood from going too low that I can't get out of it.

    What does sunlight do? Well it doesn't fix all your problems, but it helps mood by allowing human bodies to make vitamin D, and vitamin D helps the body make the brain chemicals it needs to stay balanced. If you don't get outside much like me, or you don't eat many foods that have vitamin D added to them, sitting in front of a window for a few minutes in the morning can give you what you need. Cats, by the way, get their vitamin D from food- I just find sunlight makes me feel better!

    But for the rest of your outside adventures, make sure you use a sunblock on your skin because too much sun isn't a good thing for your body either and you humans don't have built-in fur coats to protect your skin like me!

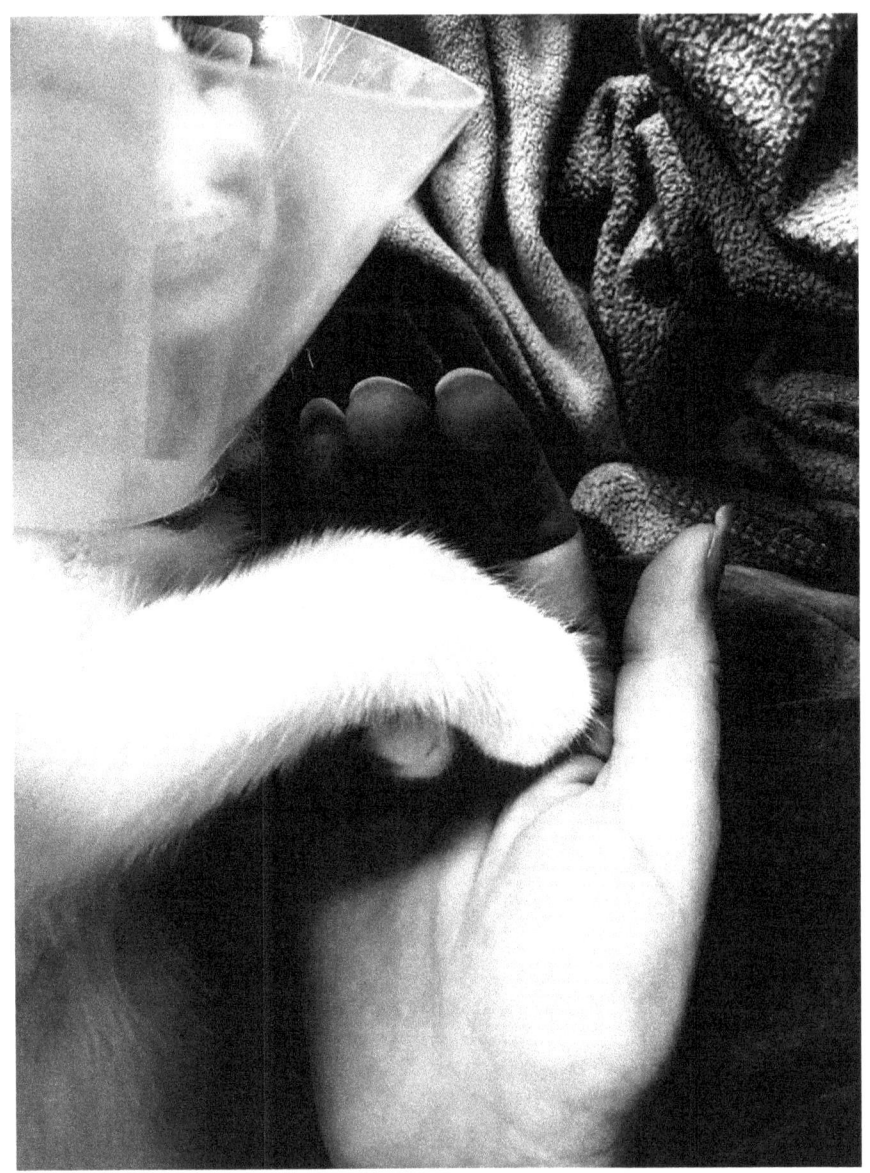

Do you know anyone who talks to a therapist?

I've heard humans telling each other they "need therapy" sometimes but they don't understand what therapy is or they would know *everyone* can use therapy once in a while. *Therapy* is talking to a professional mental health person that you trust about all sorts of stuff. You don't have to have a mental illness or take medication to talk to a therapist. Therapists are there for everyone for as long or as short a time as they are needed. It's good for our mental health to talk things out, and everyone has a problem once in a while that they need some extra help figuring out. *Therapists help you figure things out*.

Finding a therapist you get along with and trust might take a little while, because therapists are people just like everyone else and they're all different from each other. Some therapists might love cats like I do, or some might be dog people. Some might be very creative, and others might be logical. You get the idea! You just have to shop around a little. Luckily, I have my humans to talk to about my problems, but one of my humans sees a therapist all the time! And I give her therapist *four paws up*, because she really likes kittens!

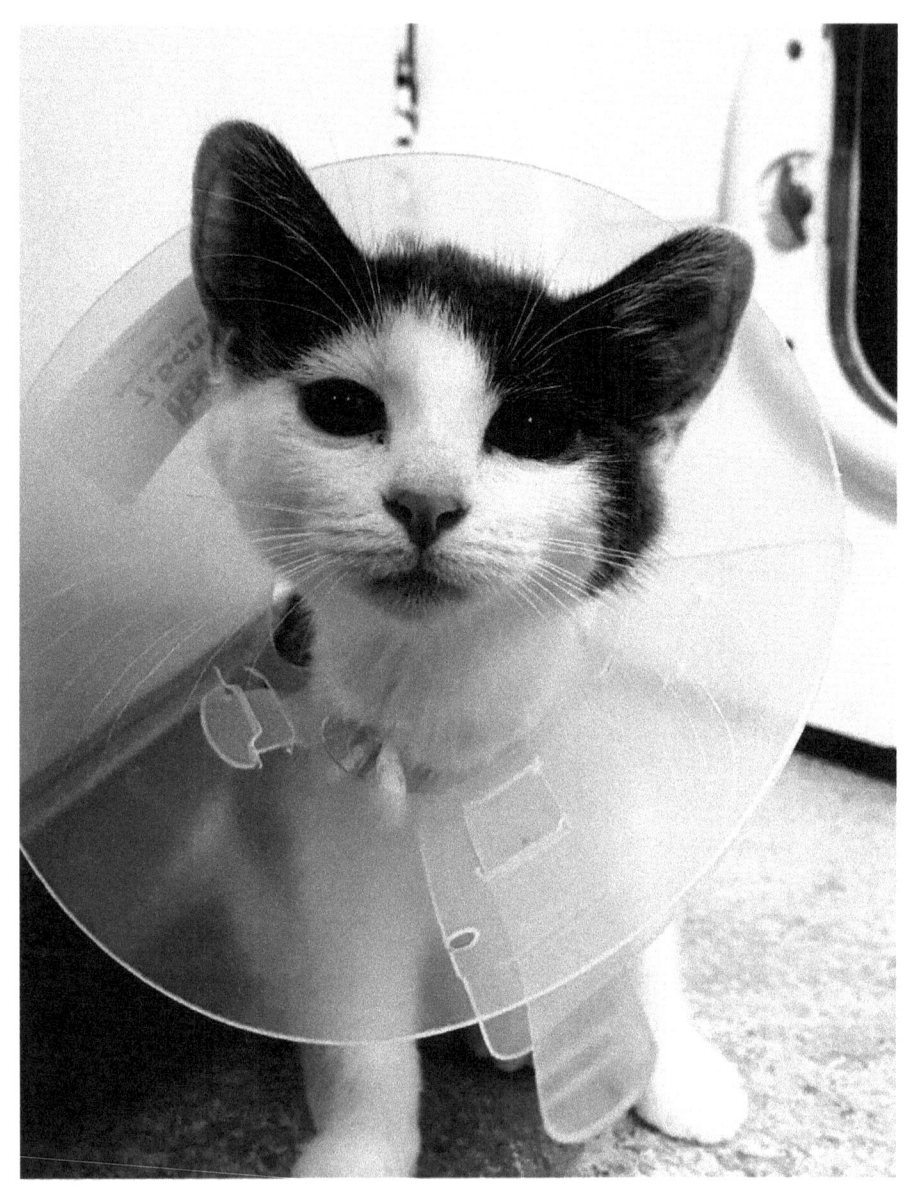

*Oh boy, did I get myself in a fix!*

This is not how I planned my day to go at all. *What had happened was*, I was minding my own business and... okay, I wasn't minding my own business and that's sort of how I got into this situation and had to go to the vet. When they put this awful collar on me, I was so angry I sat down and refused to move all evening. But then I got hungry and I couldn't figure out to reach my food. And then I cried VERY LOUD!

My human came and showed me how to eat at the edge of my bowl and she got me a big bowl of water and helped me get used to walking in my collar because I was going to have to wear it for a while. She stayed by me so I could go do the cat things I needed to do with some privacy and after a while, it wasn't so bad. I could even run and jump in it! I call this my "crown" now.

When you get into a situation you didn't plan on, you can get so angry you can't even move! Learning how to ask for help to get through it is the best thing for your mental health because it helps get your emotions under control so you can use them instead of *being used by them*. Once you get accustomed to thinking about yourself in the new situation you might even find that you can make it work. Then you can wear your own crown proudly!

I don't want to eat them; I really just want to go *play* with them.

It looks like those chickens are right beyond my reach but really, there's a window, a yard, and a fence between us! It seems pretty hopeless, doesn't it? They may as well be on the moon because I'm so little and it's so far. It was quite a climb just to get up on this table to see out of the window. But you know what? I made it all the way up on top of the table by myself. I had to climb up a chair to even get this far but *I did it*.

Sometimes our goals may seem so far away they may as well be on the moon. It can be easy to get stuck on how far you have *to go* instead of seeing how far you've *already gone*. To get where you really want to go, it's always helpful to keep *both* in mind all the time. If you only look back and see what you've done, you might get too comfortable and not go any further. And if you only look ahead to future challenges and forget your progress, you might get overwhelmed and stop right where you are too!

When I get down about how far I have to go, I think about things others have done that were really hard. Did you know that humans and cats have *both* been in space? It's true- all the way to the stars! So, then I know that if I keep on working towards my goal, there's no reason why I can't get there too!

Oh, I do love blankets! They're so soft and cozy and feel great under my paws!

When I'm stressed out, I like to do something called *self-soothing*. It's a simple way to help me calm down and feel less anxious or angry or worried. You can do it too! You just use one or more or all of your five senses.

Does touching soft things make you calm? Then get a cozy blanket like mine to knead under your fingers or steal your dog-brother's plushy toys. *I'm just kidding, ask first*!

Do sweet scents calm you down? Maybe you could burn a scented candle or sniff some perfume.

Do yummy foods make you feel better? Try a little candy or maybe some soothing tea.

Maybe music chills you out? Put on some tunes and if you feel like it, dance up and down the stairs. Just be careful kittens aren't around, 'cos we like to chase dancing feet!

Or try looking at soothing photos of flowers or patterns or *cute kittens*!

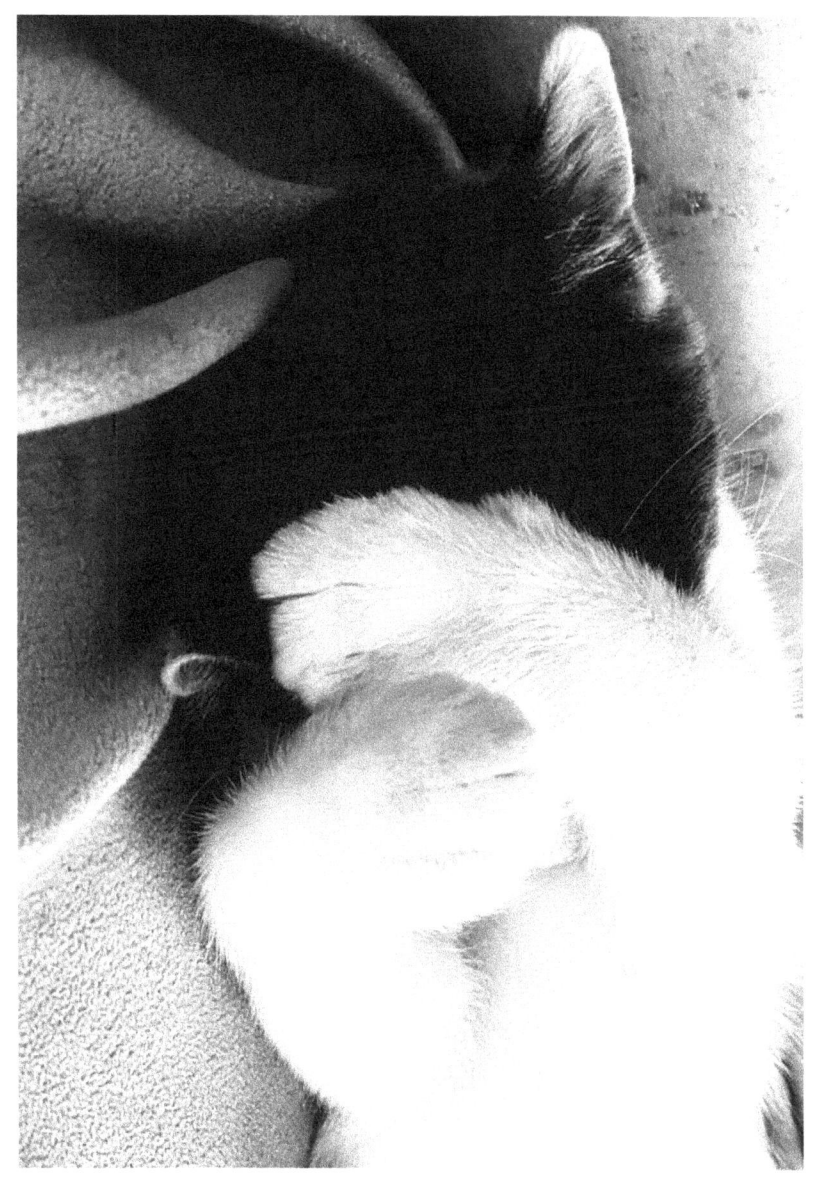

*I'm the worst kitten ever!*

My big cat-sister Aelish growled at me and my big dog-brother Orry stepped on me and my humans yelled at me when I got up on the windowsill.

Nobody likes me!

Sometimes I have to remind myself to *check my facts*. If you ever get stuck thinking the whole world doesn't like you either, try it with me:

I *don't know* that Aelish doesn't like me for sure. We played on the stairs yesterday and it was a lot of fun. Maybe she was a little sore and cranky because her back legs hurt her sometimes and she overdid it. Yeah, that's probably it.

I *don't know* that Orry doesn't like me for sure either. We worked together to catch that big horse fly the other day and we both had a great time. He's a lot bigger than me, so I bet he just didn't see me.

And *I know* my humans don't like me sitting in the window because they worry I'll fall out! There's a screen to keep me from falling but I guess they just love me a lot.

So really, I'm not the worst kitten ever, I just had a bad kitten day.

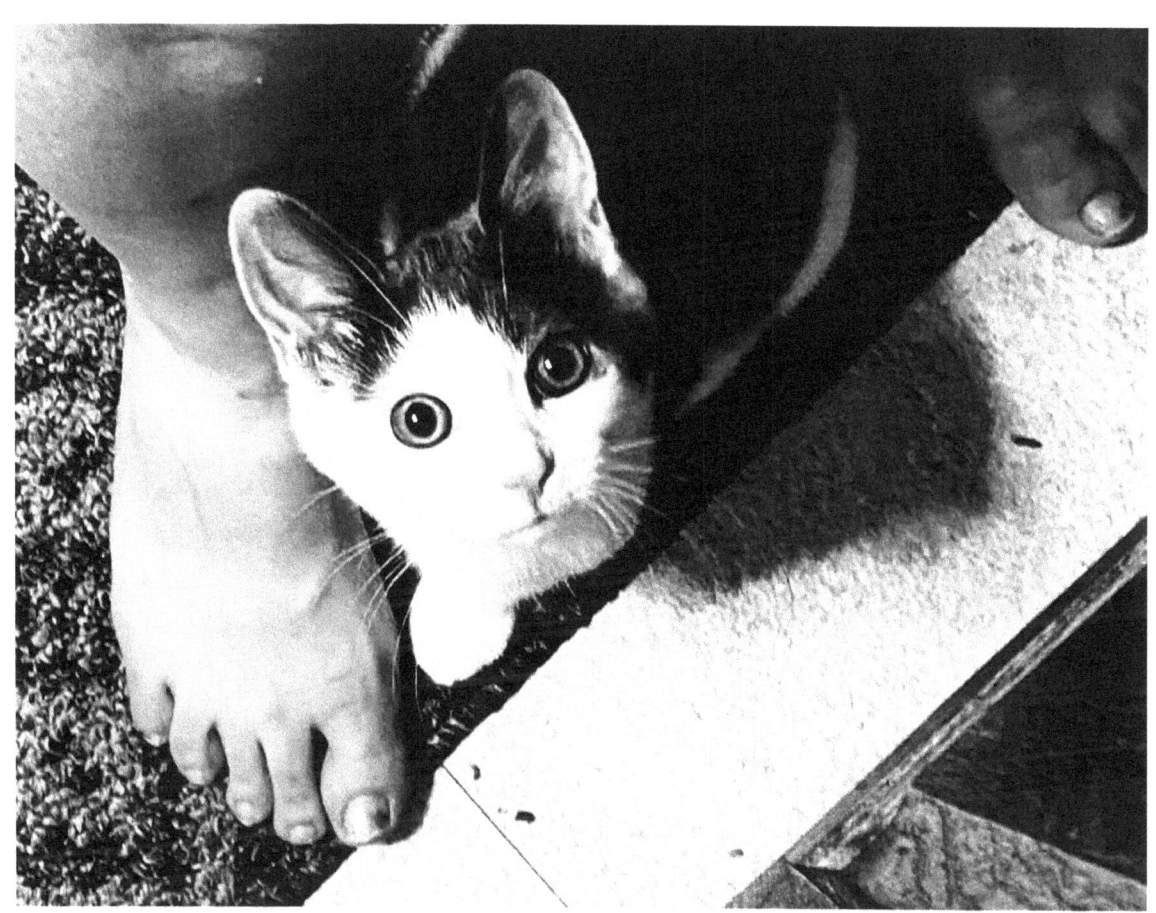

I come with back up!

Humans seem to think bullying only happens to kids, but adult humans can be bullied in their homes or workplaces or even on the bus. Even animals get bullied by other animals!

It's important to talk to someone if you're being made to feel bad about yourself or unsafe by someone else so you can try to figure out what to do about it. But don't ever go it alone- find someone you trust as backup! Trying to handle it alone doesn't work that well, does it?

I don't try to handle any big mean cats without my humans behind me. I just call us Team Skittle!

Cats are masters at sleeping and I'm practicing so I can be the best sleeper I can!

You know who else needs a lot of sleep? Humans!

Humans don't seem to ever understand how important sleep is. They're always doing more and more and *more* without stopping to get some good rest in. And sleep is really important for your mental health because when your brain is rested, it's more balanced emotionally and can handle everyday stress and make good decisions more easily.

Remember, your brain controls everything else in your body so it needs a good long break every night!

You know what kittens have in abundance?

I mean besides adorableness and fluff? We've got just *buckets* and *buckets* of confidence!

Confidence is something that's very good for your mental health. When you have confidence in yourself, you spend less time worrying and struggling with challenges. Confidence helps you feel like you can get through anything, so you're one step ahead before you even start. But how do you get confidence? They don't sell it in a store.

One way is to learn a new skill. It takes some practice but the more you work at it, the better you get, and the more confidence you build. As you can see, I've been learning to type. I'm not terribly accurate but I can confidently say I'm the fastest kitten typist on the block!

Feeling like you fit in is important no matter what species you are.

Sometimes we all feel like we don't fit in, no matter how popular or successful we may be. Sometimes I feel like I'm the only kitten in my house… well maybe that's because I am!

But I'm not the only *animal* in my house. I'm not even the only cat! It's easy to get caught up in trying to be like others to help yourself feel like you belong or comparing yourself and only looking at your differences. But I try to look for things I have in common with others while still being myself. There are four different species in my house and we *all* like to sleep in and have snacks and pile up on the couch to watch TV.

Like a puzzle, we're all different pieces that make up one big family. We can each be our own shape and still fit into a whole. Whatever group you find yourself in, remember that the group wouldn't be complete without you, and nobody else can fit in your space.

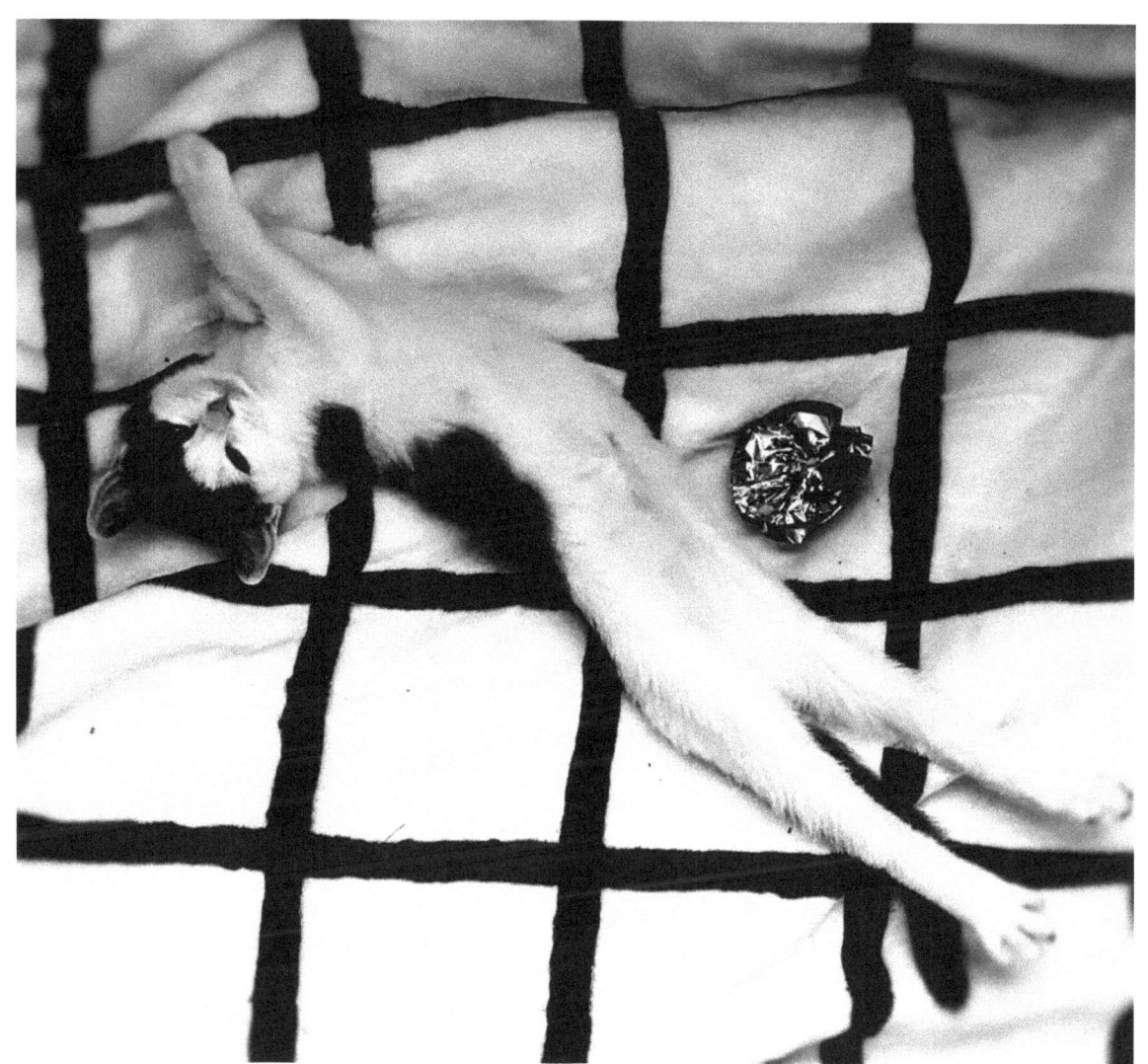

Did you know cats show their bellies to humans that they trust?

A cat's belly is their most vulnerable place ever! All our most important parts are right there in our bellies and if we ever got injured there, it could mean life or death. So, when we roll over and show our vulnerable side, we're saying *we trust you not to hurt us*.

Showing your vulnerable parts to others can be good for your mental health too. Cats might show their bellies but think about the last time you talked with someone about your hopes and fears, or about something scary that happened to you in the past. Humans become closer when they talk honestly. And when you get vulnerable with someone else, it helps you feel less anxious and more grounded because now you know you've got someone who understands on your side.

Just make sure when you share, it's with someone who's belly-worth it.

*I help!*

Helping others can really improve your mood. It gets your mind busy with thoughts other than focusing on what you're down about and gives you a little perspective. Sometimes helping others more unfortunate than you can give you a lift and help you reframe your own situation, but other times something really little and simple can make your day too.

I thought my human needed some help sewing but I found out pretty soon that paws and needles don't mix, and I *may* have gotten thread all over the place...

Turned out, my human just needed a little company, so I did my best!

I'm sure you've heard that old saying about cats and curiosity... well it is NOT true!

Cats are natural masters of curiosity and for good reason- curiosity keeps you going forward when you feel like giving up and keeps you reaching out when you feel like withdrawing. Ask yourself:

What if I tried it this way?

How else can I get there?

What else could this mean?

What if I got to...?

What does this do?

Keeping your thoughts busy with curiosity is sort of like training for your brain. It opens up your viewpoint and allows you to experience new things! Curiosity is kitten-approved!

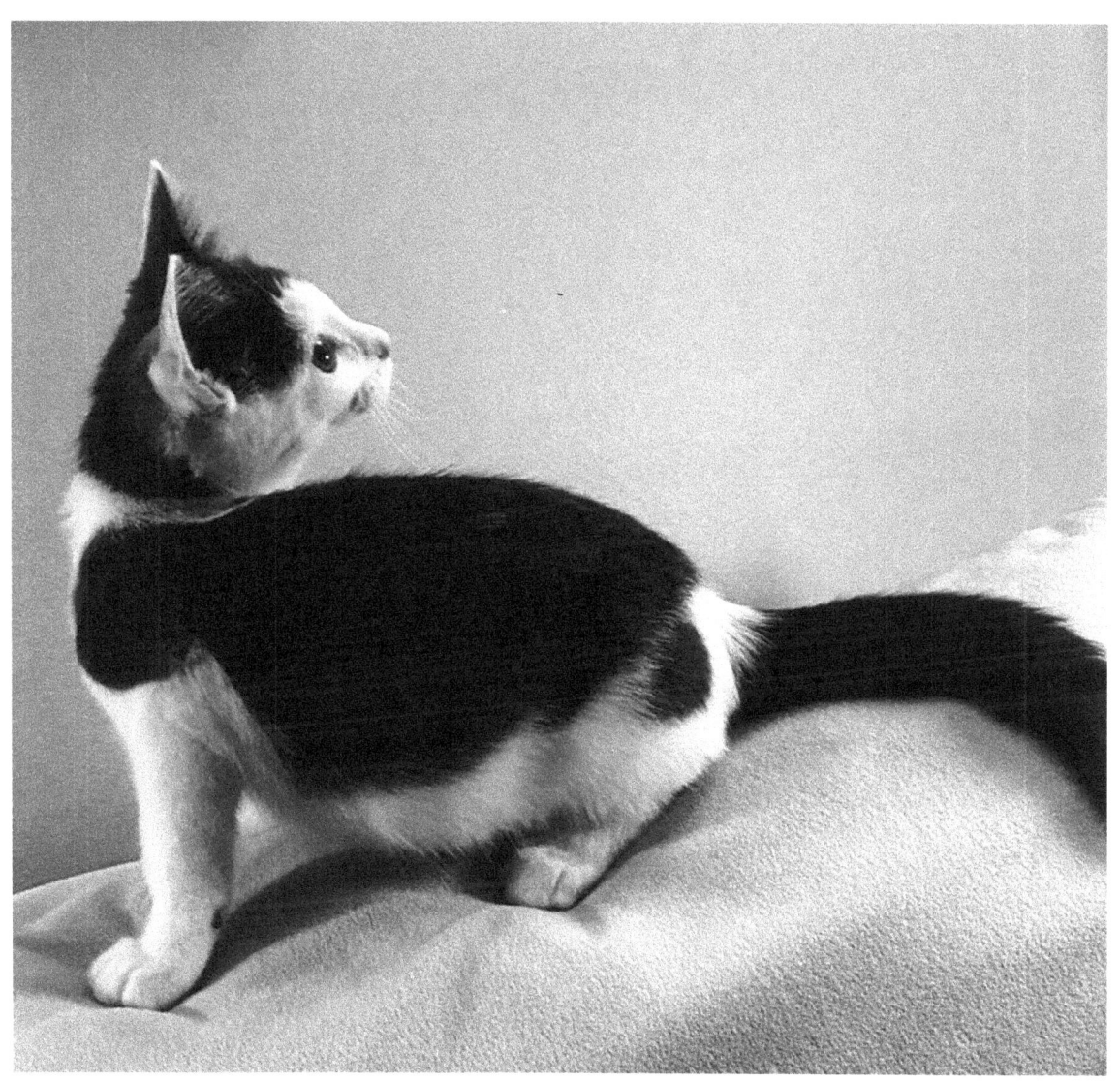

Wow, I am ready to roll!

Although my humans don't like to get up early, I make sure to get up at the same time every morning so I'm ready to face the day!

Routine is good for mental health. Getting up at the same time every morning is part of *sleep hygiene*. So is going to bed at the same time every night! These routines get your brain used to powering down and revving back up so you're less likely to have trouble getting to sleep and waking up. Set an alarm for the same time to wake up even on days you don't have to be anywhere to have the best effect.

Or get a nearby kitten to chew on your nose- we're very good at timekeeping.

*Ugh, I'm stuck!*

Sometimes you might find yourself stuck between two places you don't want to be in, and you've got to make a decision to get out of there. It's not looking good either way. So how do you decide?

Not deciding keeps you stuck and more prone to also get weighed down by anxiety or depression. One way to make a decision is by making a big list. For one choice, list all the good and bad outcomes you can think of. Repeat this for the other decision. Now look at everything you've listed. Which choice has more positive outcomes? That could very well be your answer. Of course, you can always change your mind, but at least now you've got a direction to start in to can make a smart decision and feel calmer about it.

And remember, you can *always* holler for some help. I do all the time and my humans bail me out!

*Hmm, what is this?*

I like to try new things as much as I can and it's really a good idea for your mental health to try something new once in a while. Trying new things can help you get over fears, teach your brain to handle new challenges and bring some fun and excitement into your day. Does trying new things make you anxious? Try something out with a buddy or start small!

Sometimes new things don't work out exactly as we thought they would. That's ok, we can still learn something. Take this egg for example. It looked pretty good but this hard thing on the outside made it awfully hard to eat.

Well, now I know eggs aren't my favorite food!

*Uh oh. I broke it.*

The other thing I learned about eggs is that they break!

What do I do now? My humans will be so mad!

Wait Skittle, *slow down.* It was just an accident. This is the first egg I've ever seen, so how could I know it was so easy to break? And I didn't break it on purpose, it just happened. I'll say I'm sorry and try to ask first before I take something from the counter again.

When you make mistakes, it can be easy to think bad things about yourself and then want to withdraw. But the best thing to do is apologize and remind yourself that *everyone* everywhere makes mistakes sometimes. Even kittens!

No more close-ups today!

Being the cute kitten that I am, I get a lot of photographs taken. But sometimes I need a break for a little me-time too.

Saying no is a skill everyone should have and use to keep themselves from getting too overrun with things to do and people to see. Saying no to someone or something because you don't have enough energy or time isn't being mean, it's managing your time and yourself well. If you try to do too many things at once you can't do any of them very well and after a while you may find yourself getting bitey. *Bitey* is a kitten term, it means "I'm telling you with my teeth I just can't do one more thing!"

But use your *words*. Humans don't like biting very much.

Have you ever gotten overwhelmed by something good?

If you've been having a hard time and suddenly something great happens to you, you could feel like it's too much to handle. That's not so unusual. Unexpected things can throw us for a loop and make our brains work overtime to cope. This doesn't mean you're ungrateful or you don't deserve nice things to happen to you.

One day someone gave me a big bag of toys. They were great! There were toys that crinkled and toys that rolled and toys that made noise and even toys that ran around by themselves. It was every kitten's dream come true! But it was too much all at once and I stared and stared at all those wonderful things for a long time and just couldn't enjoy them. Then I laid down and played with my tail, a kitten's natural built-in toy!

If you have to fall back on something familiar to get yourself through the stress of something new, that's ok. Take a little time out to cope and then take a second look. It only took a day or so for my cat-sister and me to have all those toys spread through the house for our humans to step on!

Growth is a funny thing isn't it?

We grow a little every day. Sometimes physically and sometimes mentally. We learn new things and have new experiences. We learn new and better ways to cope with the world around us.

But it's difficult to notice how much we're growing until we go back to an old belief or an old coping skill and find it no longer "fits" us. Sort of like my toy box. I didn't even realize I was getting bigger until I went to curl up for an afternoon nap and could barely squeeze in!

Growing means *changing*, and that can be a little scary. It may mean needing to do different things or make new friends or move somewhere new. It may mean finding a bigger box to nap in! But growing also lets us have new experiences we wouldn't have had before. I had to leave my cozy box behind, but now I'm big enough to climb up on the table and sleep in the afternoon sun. It feels so good!

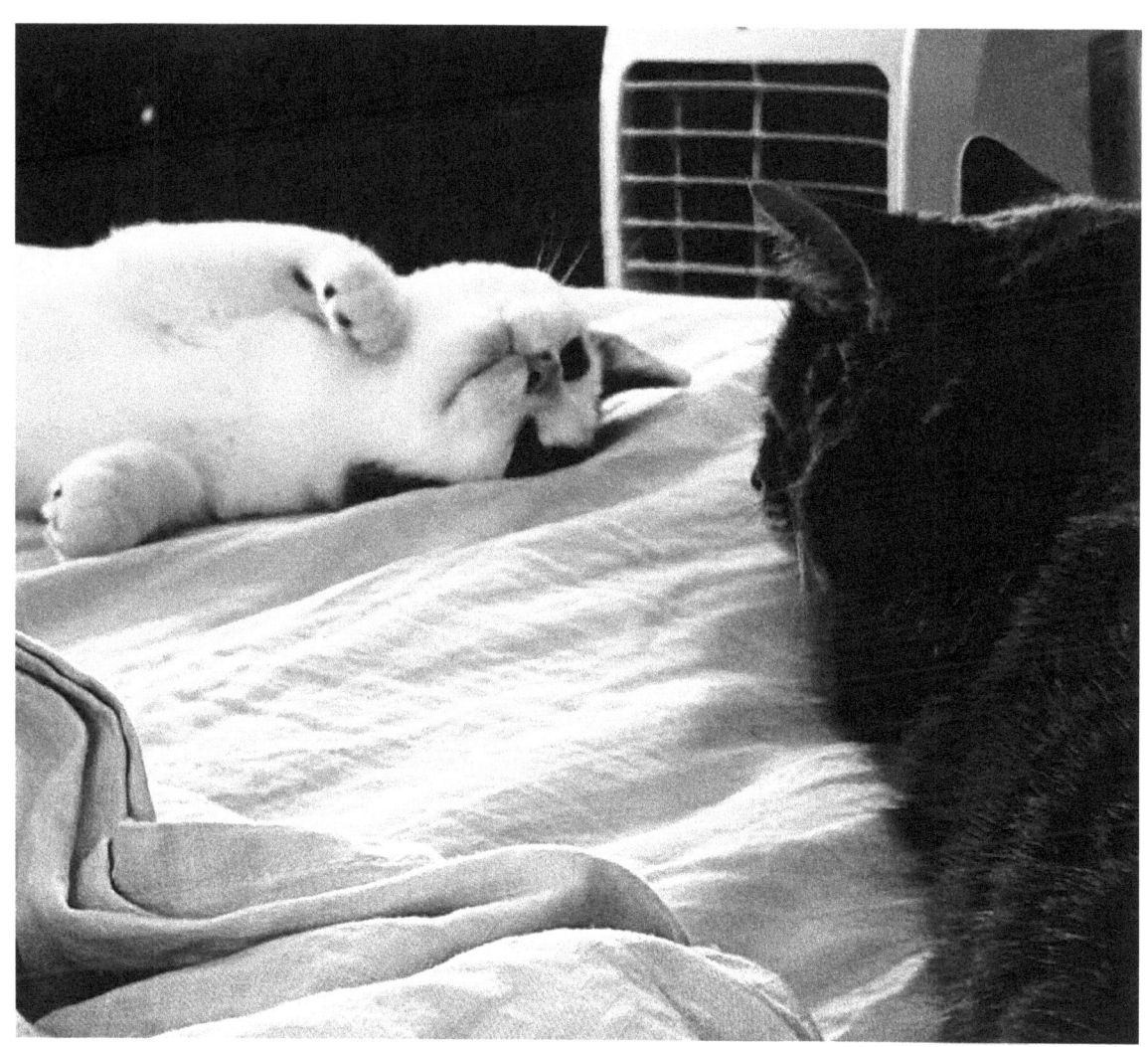

So do a kitten a favor and take care of yourself.

Keep growing and keep changing.

If you're having a rough day, grab a fellow human or animal friend to talk it over with.

Be curious, know when to say no, get your naps in, don't be too hard on yourself, always be in touch with your inner adorableness, and your brain will love you.

And kittens probably will too!

Other titles by K. Rose Quayle:

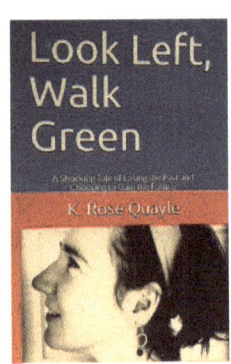  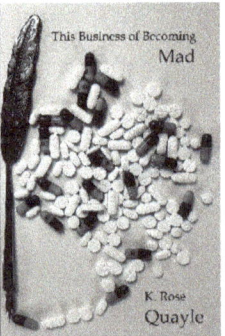

Available through Amazon.com

www.ingramcontent.com/pod-product-compliance
Lightning Source LLC
Chambersburg PA
CBHW061808290426
44109CB00031B/2964